From Shadow
to Light

Amy J Young

BookLeaf Publishing
India | USA | UK

Presentation by *BookLeaf Publishing*

Web: www.bookleafpub.com

E-mail: info@bookleafpub.com

ISBN: 9789357692311

First edition 2023

To you dear reader. I hope you continue to find the courage to move through the shadow and share the light that is you.

To my family and friends. Your encouragement has always fuelled me. Thank you. I love you.

ACKNOWLEDGEMENT

I never thought I would be a poet or publish poetry. Growing up it was just my way to express my feelings in a more creative manner. My first poems were usually about lost love or sadness. I have always been fascinated by how emotions can "jump" out of the words in a poem.

As I have grown and experienced life, so have my feelings, hence the more deeper the poems.

As I started to share my prose, friends and family often replied with similar feelings and understandings. Many suggested I share them further. So here I am. Sharing my inner deepest thoughts with you dear reader. I hope like me, you find some courage, inspiration and hope. In what can sometimes feel like a dark world full of shadows, there is always light just waiting to be seen.

I am thankful that I am surrounded by supportive family and friends. I have had much encouragement and love in my life.
A special thanks to my Dad for sharing poetry with me, my Mum for being my biggest supporter and my amazing husband for being my

rock through all of our time together. To my children and stepchildren, you bring so much light in my life that encourages me to keep going. I send so much gratitude to ALL my family and friends who are like family. To mention you all and how much you mean to me, there are not enough pages in the world for that!

And to you dear reader, thank you for taking the time to read this.

I hope you find the light within you and within these pages.

PREFACE

These poems are a little different.

I wrote them to be a creative journal documenting my journey through my shadow feelings, thoughts and actions. I used this method to remove my usual thought cycle and be able to look upon them with love and in a non-judgemental way.

Each poem reflects a healing that was needed at some point in my life. As I started to have the courage to share these poems, I found others related the words to some of their own circumstances in life.

How does one journey from shadow to light?
Let me share my journey with you.

Hidden within these poems are some of the ways I journeyed my way out of anxiety and depression. In 2005 I was first diagnosed with Anxiety however it wasn't until 2013 when it became very debilitating and changed my life forever. I was also diagnosed with Chronic Fatigue Syndrome at this point.

I had a deeper knowing that these were the symptoms of something else that was going on under my surface.

From there I began my journey inward to start the long process of unraveling myself. The answers would come to me in words, lines and prose. They would spill out of me onto the page and I would read them back to find the answers I was seeking. Coincidence? I don't think so. I believe we all have the answers within, it just may not look the same for everyone. It did take a lot of practice for me to learn how to still the mind and work with the heart in order to reach this knowledge. I am still practicing to this day! But the more I do this, the deeper I go.

It takes work to unlearn old habits and create new ones. Often we need to look deeper as to why we learned those habits in the first place before we can truly change. Otherwise, you may find yourself repeating the same pattern! The best advice someone gave to me was that "there are two sides to every story". I have used this as a guide to look at my stories and look at ALL sides of it! Hence why these poems are often in the third person.

I hope you enjoy reading my poems. Maybe some similarities in your life or someone you know? Either way, I am so thankful for your time.

With love,

Amy

I AM

I am LOVE
Not only when I choose to feel it

I am LIGHT
Not only when I choose to see it

I am ALIVE
Not only when I choose to remember it

Time

Remember a time
When the time was more simple
Time was not kept
But measured with moments

Time was not thought of
Only used as a guide
To know the change of seasons
To read the rising of the tides

If time could openly speak
What would it want to say
Would it like being trapped
On a wrist all day

Would it enjoy being told
There is never enough
Would it feel hurt to know
It's labelled a thief of the heart

Would time be ok knowing
It is on everyone's mind
Chasing and demanding
More or less of its kind

Go fast or go slow
Time can't get it right
Everyone has time
In their plea and their plight

If only I had more time
To spend being with you
Why does time feel so wasted
In a line or a queue

I can't wait to the time
I am happy and free
How long must I work
To get time just for me

If time could speak
I'm sure it would say
Don't wait for tomorrow
Live only for today

I am simple if you only just let me be
Stop living your life on your need for me

Turn away from my numbers
Stop racing my pace
See me in nature in my natural state
I will show you the way I came to be
I only wanted to guide you to live in harmony

See me in the sunrise and as the sun sets
I will leave you breathless and feeling content
See me in the smile of a newborn babe
See me in the smile of a person of any age

I should only be measured in moments of life
I am not here to chase you
I am not here to cause strife

I have given you this gift
So please use me lovingly
I want to journey alongside you
Collecting only your memories

And I will keep them safe
As treasures always retraced
And carry them through lifetimes
Alive forever
In a timeless embrace.

A Kind Stranger

"How are you?" they would say
"I'm good" she will reply
Ignoring all the pain inside
Hiding behind a smile so wide
Thinking no one could depict
Her lies so white.

A kind stranger would watch her
As she passed them by
And would smile to her warmly
And step to the side.
Each day they would notice
The girl's usual reply
And humbly wonder
What the girl's life was like.

The girl living a life
With days on repeat
Fading away
Into looping weeks.
The years forming lines
In crevices above her cheeks
She struggled through the day
With nights of no sleep.
She felt stuck.

She felt sad.
She did not understand why
Freedom felt like a dream made of lies.
She looks in the mirror and avoids her eyes
Because she knows all she will see is the truth
she hides.
Each day she applies her mask of smiles
So she could feel safe
And hide her feelings of denial.

One day a kind stranger pulled her near
Leaning in whispering slowly and clear
"I see you" "It's ok" "Let go of the tears"
"I see all the signs"
"I see all the fear"
"Because smiles were a mask
I too hid behind
From experiences of past
I had suffered a similar kind"

The kind stranger opened their arms warm and
wide
So the girl felt held and safe to cry.
The stranger proclaimed while holding her close
"These are the days we need hugs the most"
"I might be a stranger
But I have love to share
Because thanks to my own past
When I found solace in another's care"

"You may feel alone
You may feel this is it
But I'm here to tell you
You will get passed this bit.
It's ok to feel sad.
To feel angry.
To cry!
It's ok to let go of the feelings bottled up inside.
It's ok to be where you are at this time
Let me help you to seek within and find
All the answers held safely
Within your heart confined"

"I know not your past
Or the journey you walk
But I am here to listen and to let you talk.
No judgement from me
I will listen carefully
And offer only that
Which you feel you will need"

"I understand how it feels to be trapped.
I want you to know that I can share that fact.
Our journeys may differ
and so too the reasons we hide
But together we can help one another to climb
Out of the darkness
Out of the hole

Let me stand beside you
With strength and soul.
I too made the climb
And not on my own
As I had a kind stranger
Help me from feeling alone"

The girl thanked the stranger
And felt a warm light
As it lit a warm ember
Within her body that night.
She slept more soundly
And finally felt
That the hole had grown smaller
As the darkness began to melt.

All it took was a kind person to reach out a hand
Which gave her reason to understand
There is hope in this moment
And it's ok to share
A healing path
In another's care.
And the girl finally felt
That one day she would be fine
And just maybe she too
Could be someone's kind stranger in time.

Dear Anxiety

I have a friend named anxiety
She often likes to sit with me

Her body is hunched
Worry written on her face
She sways ever so slowly
Gazing out into space

I ask her to tell me all the things on her mind
She looks at me fearfully with pain-filled eyes

I open my arms and I hold her there
She slides into panic and utters words of despair

She worries about the past with so much sorrow
She worries about the impact it will have on
tomorrow

She tries to think rationally and be one step
ahead
In preparation for all the outcomes held in her
head

It has all become too much
She is drowning in stress

She wants to run and hide
And be free of this mess

As her breath becomes rapid
I ask her to slow
She shakes her head angrily
And explains how it goes

Her heart beats too fast
Her throat is so dry
Her body feels heavy
Her eyes try to cry
But she cannot move
Her feet chained to the ground
She can no longer hear
She can't make a sound

I see her mind thinking
Spiralling fast
She is deciding her next move
Fight or flight is her path

I hold her hand tight
And put her hand on my heart
I tell her this is the best place to start

I hold her gaze strong
And invite her to breathe
Her hand on my heart

Feels the rhythm she needs

I show her this moment
The presence of now
She settles into her body
As it breathes in and out

We find where anxiety
In her body is stored
We breathe fresh air into its energetic core

We acknowledge that anxiety
Is an emotion so real
But all it wants is for the body
To be still and to feel

As we feel it together
And ask it why
It starts to respond
And we finally cry

A release of the stress
That was hiding so deep
But once it was acknowledged
It could now be released

The mind is so strong
But needed a rest
The heart tried to tell it

But the head thought it knew best

Anxiety had wanted to help everyone
By holding their worries so they could have fun
She sheltered those around her from pain and
from fear
And held it to her close
So she could save all their tears

But as she held them
one by one
Her body would become
more overrun
Until one day her body had had enough
She would no longer feel joy
and no longer feel love
Anxiety screamed and finally released
All the pain she had held
With every heartbeat

It was ok to offer others her help
but only after she had taken care of herself
If she filled her own cup
She would have plenty to share
As long as she replenished it
With self-love and self-care

I hugged my friend anxiety
And told her I was proud

For this loving new knowledge
that she had courageously found
I whispered
Remember…
If you ever feel down…
All you need is to breathe in this moment…
Right now

Seasons Cycles of Life

SPRING
Springing from the sun a shiny new life
Purity of love and child innocence
Rebellious joy and naive strife
Invigorating in life's consonance
Nurtured by others with freedom and love
Gratitude for having more than enough

SUMMER
Stepping out bravely on one's own
Using love's pulse as a guide
Meeting partners and seeds being sown
Mending broken hearts at night
Enjoying a sunkissed body of love
Radiating in the warm balmy light

AUTUMN
Adapting as the body creates and changes
Ushering in new life through love with another
Turning to greet new spring faces
Understanding life through the eyes of a mother
Making home and hay in safe places
Nurturing a growing family with love

WINTER
Welcoming the change in the tapestry of life
Inviting an ear to share life's advice
Nuancing the freedom of a life now grown
Thankful to memories of love when shown
Enjoying a reminisce of a springtime wonder
Ready to return to the sun's embrace once more

Dear Fear

Dear Fear
Hold me near
Keep me safe
In your arms of despair

Keep my light tightly locked away
Safe from forces that like to play
In a playground of my thoughts they like to
climb
Holding me back so I don't shine

Fear whispers to me of a safe domain
Hiding within a bloodless vain
Locked in a space that feels like home
Using its guise to stay in the known

Fear whispers to me so softly and sweet
Leading me gently away to retreat
To a cell located in only my mind
No light can be stolen within its confines
"Keep your light safe and you will be fine"
"Keep it locked tight in these safe walls of mine"

"There is a force that calls itself Love" warned
Fear

"It will try to tempt you away from here"

"Don't listen to love"
Fear repeats with haste.
"Better to not feel,
What love wants you to taste"

"But love sounds so sincere?"
I question you Fear

"Why do you not want my light to be shared?
Why do you hold me so tight and keep me
unaware?
Why do I have to stay locked away?
Why can't I dance and sing and play?
Why must I dim this light for you Fear?
Why is staying safe the only reason you care?

What if Love can also keep my light safe?
Keeping it open and not locked in a cage.
Showing me a way to share its delight,
Showing me a way to use it that feels right!
What if by sharing I become someone new?
And I remember a feeling that treats me different
to you!?"

"Thank you Fear
You have taught me so much!

But now I must stop using you as my
thoughtless crutch
Love has shown me a way that feels so true
A safety I can bask in that feels more safer than
you!
I no longer hold the hand that holds me back
I reach for the light that keeps me from lack
No longer confined in a thoughtless mind
But open to possibilities of the unlimited kind"

"Fear I love you,
Without you I would never have grown
To feel this true love all on my own"

"Fear, you are safe with ME within my light
It never dims
It always shines bright
Love will protect us
Both you and me
All we need to do is trust and be free

My teacher, my shadow, my companion, my
friend
Fear please take my hand
I won't leave you behind
Love will hold both of us
We don't need to hide
There is more than enough
 For both of us to fly

Away from the cell no longer confined!"

Side by side we will rise
Out from the ashes
No longer fear, Fear
For love will always catch us.

A Dream

I opened my eyes this morning
Too early for the sun
Awakened from a dream
Where emotions had become overrun

In my dream I had been wandering
Familiar scenes but places unknown
Conversing with silent faceless people
With feelings, colours and tones

From colours so bright and vivid
Disappearing to darker shades of grey
My pace became more quickened
As dream's night hastily befell the day

My wandering turned to a frightful chase
As I felt the darkness overcome
A faceless figure pursued me
But my body felt paralysed and numb

As I fell to the ground powerless
I succumbed to its energetic blow
Feeling defeated and defenceless
I turned bravely to face my foe

The shape shifted to big round eyes
With a stare so familiar and real
I cried out in surprise
As its identity slowly became revealed…..

***

I opened my eyes this morning
Too early for the sun
Awakened from an intense dream
Where emotions had become overrun

As my mind slowly adjusted
From my somber disarray
I slowly started to piece together
The reality of the day

Searching for a meaning
Of a dream turned nightmare
The shadow's eyes etched in my memory
I scrambled to place its familiar stare

As the sun arose it dawned on me
Running to a mirror so I could see
The fear I had been running from
It's eyes…
Reflecting…
Back at me…

Path of Shadows

Let me tell you a story
About a journey you must make
An adventure we all must one day partake
No one escapes
We all follow this fate
In our own divine time
There is no jumping the line

Away from your home within my light
Into the darkness of the darkest night
You will courageously step
Where your curiosity will be met
By a path in the shadows
No not where it goes
No not where it ends
Take a deep breath
And dive on in

The path may be dark
It may be at times so frightening
Just have faith
And know each step will be taken rightly

Do not fear
I am still by your side

As your conscious
I will be your heart-filled guide
Like a lighthouse
I will hold the light for you
Through the darkness
Down the path of truth
Holding your hand
You don't have to feel alone
We will battle faceless forces
And with each step you will grow
The path will get easier
Lighter as you go
The more you trust
with more ease it will flow

You will begin to realise
The darkness was wise
Your thoughts of separation
Were your only demise
The light was always there
You only had to see
That all that you wanted
And all that you need
Was hidden in plain sight
Within your own internal light

So with this awakening
From your adventurous sleep
The path will turn infinite

In all answers you seek

Lit up like gold
The shadows all gone
Your being will be full
Abundance will unfold
Surrounded in beauty
to breathtakingly behold

And as this story comes
full circle once more
You will realise what your journey
was worth taking for
To experience an adventure
to truly learn what love is
You had to leave your home of safety
And seek darkness for this

So when you have had
The time of your life
You will return back to me
Forever free
to be loved in my light
For eternity

Is this the life I signed up for?

Towing the line
Trying to find
A way out of the ego's bind
Its grasp on my mind
Keeping my nose to the grind
Afraid to lose my place in the line
When will life be mine
No longer a hard climb
Living by my own design
It ain't the kind
Of life I signed
Up for - Or did I?

Take a fallback
Off the treadmill track
Reeling from scarcity and feeling of lack
Falling into a heavy heaped stack
Rock bottom fades to the darkest black
Wide open I crack
Surrender to slack
There's no way I am turning back
It ain't the kind
of life I signed
up for - Or did I?

Feelings deranged
Life has now changed
No longer caged
Ego's thoughts rearranged
Living life in a brand new way
No longer tamed
A design of my own game
Abundance gained
Love permanently ingrained
Now this is the kind of life
I signed up for
Or did I?

As I watch and rewind
The truth I will find
About life's cycle
to fall and to climb
Was cleverly designed
To express soul's infinite heart and mind
No longer be blind
To ego's design
There is no existence of a daily grind
To yourself and others just always be kind
Love is life's treasure to unwrap and find
This is the kind of life
I signed up for…

I promise to remember and embrace it this time.

Dear Anger

I have a friend named Anger
She has been visiting of late
I have asked her numerous times
To not visit me in this state

She doesn't listen to reason
She won't readily stop her wrath
She only wants to erupt with force
And hold me in her iron clasp

I feel when she is ever so close
And I try to push away
But once she has me in her sight
She will control me for the day

She turns up when I least expect
Or when I'm feeling trapped
She explodes ever so quickly
In her rage, I am tightly wrapped

One day I felt so ashamed
As she had taken charge again
She had burst into heated flames
Leaving behind a destructive trail of blame

As the tears of defeat ran down my face
I courageously asked her near
I asked her why she acted this way
I dared her to be truthful and clear

She looked at me surprised
As I caught her unaware
She hung her head towards her toes
And asked me why I cared

I placed my arm around her
And pulled her to me close
I whispered soft and slowly
"Because I only want to grow"

She told me her real name was sadness
And she had tried to let it known
She said "you always ignore me"
"I had nowhere else to go"

"The more you ran away from me
The louder I would get
Hoping that one day soon
My needs would finally be met"

"You may recall the time
My heart had broken into two
All I wanted was to grieve and cry
All I wanted was to be felt by you"

"You asked me to stay away
The pain was too much to bare
You locked me in your heart confined
And left me alone in there"

"I waited in the darkness
For the day we could finally grieve
But you piled more feelings on top of me
I burst out of the seams"

I am most often misunderstood
And I only need to be loved
I am sadness growing to despair
When I have finally had enough"

"I can tell you what you need to grow
Please listen carefully
Grieving when sad is paramount
And feeling is our reprieve"

"I know it hurts to feel it all
And pain can be too much to know
But letting it out
Instead of bottling it in
Will help keep our feelings in flow"

"From time to time you may call on me
As anger and as friends

Our trail can be left with feelings of love
And not full of bitter ends"

"Seek solace when I need you
And shower me with love
Let's work together
To understand
So together we rise above"

"Thank you for being so brave
To finally speak to me
I know how hard it is to look
But now I'm finally free"

I thanked anger for her truth
I forgave her then and there
I turned the forgiveness to myself
And promised myself self-care

And in the future if and when
Anger visits me again
I will welcome her with kindness
And with love for my lifelong friend.

Rebirth

No longer fit for this world or this time
Time to adventure outside this glasshouse of
mine

Your eyes may no longer
hold me within
but your heart will feel me
through thoughts I am in

Times have changed
and so too must we
As change is written
in our lives constantly

I will reside in your heart and keep it warm
I will sit beside you as you gently mourn
I will embrace your arms when you cross them
so tight
I will soften your fists when you clench them to
fight
I will gently kiss the frown on your head
I will sing you a lullaby when you rest in your
bed

I will always be with you

Our past not too far gone
And I will cheer for you
as you adventure on

We have journeyed this far
But it's now time to go
It's time to learn
Spread your wings and grow

And as you hold
your head up high
I will journey alongside you
Into your new life…

Dear Friend

One day I felt so lonely
I felt like I was on my own
I had no one checking in on me
I had no calls on the telephone

I thought about the friends I have
And wondered where they had gone
Had I done something to upset them
Had I said something that was wrong

It had been some time since we last spoke
Sometime since our last connect
Did they disappear
And leave me here
On my own to self reflect

I thought about them individually
I thought about them the things I like
I wondered what they were doing right now
And did they know I was missing from their life

And as I listed and counted their qualities
Their perfect imperfect quirks
I smiled at our warmest memories
And let go of my self-imposed hurt

It dawned on me that I had been
The one to go within
I had focussed on my own well being
And had not even clued them in

I called a dear friend to talk to them
And shared thoughts of my dismay
She reflected with feelings in her own life
And my call had made her day

We both had become so consumed
In our feelings of being alone
We had forgotten to remember to share the load
With the people who care the most

We cleared the space lovingly
And held each other's feelings tight
We promised to stay open without judgement
And be one another's light

We don't have to be alone
We just need to be vulnerable to share
Know that a true friend is ready to listen
And be ready to return the care

So to the friends you hold so dearly
They are the ones worth fighting for
As friendships are here to remind us

They give life so much more

…Connect with someone today…

Awakened

It's Time
To rhyme
Step up to the lime
Light
And fight
For my right
To choose
Who to be
And I have chosen me
Time to be
The one I see
In the mirror
Of smoke
That finally cleared
The one I had always feared
Who I saw through the tears
Just a girl
With her eyes on the world
Her life ready to unfold

Time to take a chance
Stand up and dance
And speak the words
Needing to be heard

Thought it was over
Thought I was done
But looked in the mirror
To see that I've won
The greatest prize of all
And that's to be alive!

From rock bottom
I have learnt to survive
Time to revive
My soul that was hushed
And told to be quiet
Told not to fuss
But finally my ego's
getting too weak
To control the show
And hide the real me
It once held me back
But now that I've cracked
There's no turning back

I found my answers
My truth
My soul
Time to finally bless this hole
The hole in my heart
That the ego had told
Was nothing but hate and greed and pride
It lied

Told me it was safe to believe
Come to me for relief
But in the end
it only led me to fear
It tried
Offered bribes
Seduced me with lies
Wanted my all
Wanted suicide

Showed me a world full of hate
But now I see clearly
My ego is too late
I've chosen my soul
Time to fill that hole
With a universe of magic
Deep down inside
All I had to do was
Sit and try
Try to connect
In my heart
Is where to start
And learn it's right here
Has been all along
Not outside
Or in ego's song

And when I tune in
It whispers a truth

Love always wins
For those who trust
You are more than enough

So it's time to change
And not let the pain
Try to refrain
From what I have to say
You can do the same
Live only for today
Show others they too
Can learn how to play
In a life without chains
It's time to be conscious
It is time to awake
For all beings sake

Yesterday is gone
Tomorrow's not certain
Time to stop living behind the curtains
Take center stage
Step into your light
Show the world you are no longer
Scared to fight
For your right

To life
To love
To all of the above

Wake up now
It's your turn to shine

Dear Regret

My feelings of regret
Call on me when I try to forget
About times of past
I no longer want to know
Its presence reminds me
of paths I wish I had chosen

I want to move forward
But my memory's grasp is so tight
I want to be excited
For a new present and future life

I wish I was free
Like I was before
Would it be easier now
Had I chosen a different door

Had I said all the things
That had remained unsaid
Would I be less of this feeling
Stuck in a loop in my head

As I long for a time
That I can't seem to let go
I cry out in anguish

For the past to leave me alone

And as the feelings once more
Repeat the patterns I have known
It finally dawns on me
Is regret part of my growth?

Had I done all the things
I had simply regret
Would I still have repeated them
Until the lessons were met?

Maybe regret is simply not regret at all
But a wheel of fortune
Ready to spin to the pattern once more

Giving me the chance
to choose differently this time
Not to hold on to the past
But use it as a compass and guide

When I open my eyes
Using regret as my new light
New paths and opportunities
Illuminate in plain sight

Focussing only on my past
I had failed to see
Ways I could rewrite them

Were simply waiting in present time for me

I now have the chance
To learn at last
It was only my perspective
Who held tight to the past

Now that I understand
Patterns cycle around once more
I can try again
And choose different from before

With this new awareness
I no longer grasp the past so tight
I can look back on it more fondly
And thank regret for returning me
from shadow to light

Kindness

I will plant a seed of kindness
Deep within a soil rich in love
I will water it with gratitude
And watch with hope from the ground above

I will sing to it words of praise
As I wait patiently for it to grow
I will keep it safe with humility
And warm it with a gentle heartfelt glow

I will humbly encourage it daily
To rise out of the ground
From its cocoon in the darkness
It will journey safe and sound

And when the divine time comes
For it to seek the world above
I will welcome it with open arms
And shower it with unconditional love

To the heavens it will continue to grow
Boldly, beautiful and true
I will sit under its compassionate reach
And be moved by its benevolent view

In times when the outside world gets me down
I will heed comfort in its grace
And remember how a small seed of kindness
Grew to an infinite altruistic embrace

I Now See It

Now I see it
The LIGHT
Peeking above the horizon and welcoming in the
new day

Now I see it
The LIGHT
Within the sparkle of joy-filled eyes
On the brink of every smile
Interloped within the sound of every sweetly
spoken word

Now I see it
The LIGHT
Exchanged between a hug
A lovers embrace
Within the melodic movement of a child at play

Now I see it
The LIGHT
Dancing amidst the notes
of a song sung with hope
Warming the corners of a heart-shaped box
And gently caressing the lining of a reminiscent
happy memory

But most surprisingly
Now I see it
The LIGHT
In the mirror reflecting back to me
In my tears
In my smile
Within each heartbeat
And riding the wave of my every breath

Now I see it
The LIGHT
In you
And finally in me

Dawn

It's beautiful here…

Safe
Sitting in the shadows
Watching
Waiting
Biding my time

Protected in the dark
I can move without being seen
I can hide ever so easily
Watching from the outskirts

I watch the light slowly
Making its presence known
In grandeur it peeks
Over the horizon
Scanning the shadows
Looking for life

I reach out hesitantly
Slowly
Curiously
The light draws me in
But I stand frozen

Safe in the darkness

The light
Slowly seeps in
Illuminating each dark area
With a soft warmth
Slowly beckoning
The shadow to dissolve

Warming the hand
Warming the body
Finding a home to settle
Within the heart

Hopeful
I step forward
Engulfed in radiance
Bathed in light

The shadows
Lovingly
Open their arms to the light
As they dissolve
From darkness to grey
To stunning hues of gold

Safety
Turns to confidence
To freedom

To love

Even the darkest of nights
Will dissolve in the light

From Shadow to Light

From the flames I rise
The ashes still smoulding
But new visions I'm holding
As my wings are unfolding
As I rise from the fire
Towards new desires
As my spirit takes flight
Reaching new heights
I soar
I roar
To realms I have never been before
Shatter the glass ceiling
No words for what I'm feeling
I'm awake and not dreaming
The moment is here
The one that I feared
I would never be near
The one that I thought
would never appear
And now it unfolds
A new chapter to behold
A journey of a dark night
Ending with the brightest light
Back down to earth
Feelings of mirth

A new dawn
A new day
A new life to play
Watching the sun chase
The shadows away
I expand as I breathe
A new life
A new belief
Tears of joy
Stream down my face
Love has a new home
In my heart it will grace
Leaving no trace
Of an old life's state
For now I am open
To love eloping
My entire being
I'm feeling
I'm seeing
I'm finally living
And I'm ready to be
All of Me…